INTRODUCTION

By Wendy Molyneux, The He

My daughter Evie had a tough time at Junior School leading to severe anxiety throughout her teens. Inspired by trying to help her, I discovered and trained to teach the "Law of Attraction" or "Magical Magnetising". I call it that because you use it to "magic-up" things that you want. Evie used it to get a starring role in a big local theatre show. This was a lightbulb moment for me – children, teenagers, everyone can use Magical Magnetising, and the earlier you start the better. I want every child to have this magic, to use it to live a life that makes them feel light and happy, and to share it with their loved ones too. This is a "get alongside" book – parents can role model it to their children, and children can teach parents.

Image Thank You – Olga Almukhametova

Inspired & Co-Edited by Evie Molyneux

This is the book that I wish had existed for my lovely daughter to help her at a younger age to be more resilient, calmer, and ultimately happy which is all we want for our kids. I could not be prouder of her beautiful soul, creative talent, and brilliant writing skills. She helped me to co-edit this book.

Design Concept by Freddie Molyneux.

My wonderful son has always been a lucky boy who seems to magic-up a great life. He expects life to be good and generally it is – he is a natural user of Magical Magnetising without really being aware of it. He is a self-taught graphic designer, always loving to sit and create from a young age (usually football shirt designs!)

Front Cover Design

Thank you to William Potter for the magical green heart that leapt out to me as the front cover image.

ISBN: 9798769577895

Foreword by Jo Fenton. Primary School Science Teacher of the Year, Head of Year, and Pastoral Lead at Orchard Junior School.

In over twenty-five years of primary education, I have observed that no well-meaning learning interventions work for a child unless they are in a good place to learn. Unless they are safe, secure, and confident within themselves, it is hard for even the most talented teacher to help a child make progress. When we make strides in emotional stability, or even baby steps, that's when the learning takes place, and the calm replaces anxiety, smiles replace fear, and learning becomes embedded and meaningful. That's why I do my job.

Sadly, an ever-increasing number of children, young people and parents are struggling with anxiety. Unless tackled, this can spiral out of control and lead to more significant mental-health issues, non-attendance in school and whole families struggling to cope.

This book gives children and parents alike a magic toolbox to handle the worries, fears, and doubts that we all have. Whether you suffer from anxiety, self-doubt, low self-esteem or simply need a little 'pick up', "Magical Me" is an absolute must. It gives you the magic wand of permission to be yourself - the very best version of yourself. Clearly written it takes very little effort to read. Wendy simplifies the complex, whilst making you stop and think.

Kids – it's a book you can snuggle up on your bed with when you come in from school and need a bit of a boost. Take your time and come back to it again and again. So many of the suggestions can be used anytime, anyplace. Literally have them up your sleeve, like a magic wand, for those moments of worry.

A special note about "the Universe" All faiths and belief systems are welcome in my life, and I have great respect for the right to choose. If "Universe" isn't in line with your beliefs and doesn't feel right to you, please replace it with God, Source, Buddha, Allah or the word or phrase that represents your own devotional energy.

Lastly, have a "Magical Me Journal" It is a good idea to have a nice "Magical Me Journal" and pen handy (or an exercise book which you could decorate) as there are a few things you might want to write down as you go through this book.

I really hope that you enjoy "Magical Me" and come back to it time and time again. Please spread the love and tell your friends about it too. Parents and carers you will find more about Heartfulness and help for you on my website or Heartfulness Facebook page or drop me an email.

Wendy xxx
The Heartfulness Coach™
wendy@heartfulnesscoaching.co.uk
https://heartfulnesscoaching.co.uk/
https://www.facebook.com/theheartfulnesscoach

MAGICAL ME CONTENTS

CHAPTER 1 - A LIFE THAT MAKES YOU FEEL LIGHT AND HAPPY
Connect with the power that makes your dreams come true. An introduction to MAGICAL FINGER-TAPS.

CHAPTER 2 - IT'S THE LAW!
The History and Science of the Law of Attraction and the Famous People that use it. An important word about Mis-Takes.

CHAPTER 3 - THE MAGIC MAGNET INSIDE YOU
The Power of Love. Help yourself with Heartful Breathing + Heart Anchoring + Acupressure for Anxiety.

CHAPTER 4 – GOODBYE UNHAPPY THOUGHTS
Learn how to stand up to your "Little Voice". Your "Monkey Mind". Say Hello to Happy Thoughts and try a Negativity Clean Up.

CHAPTER 5 - POSITIVE THOUGHTS ATTRACT POSITIVE THINGS
Use Positive Phrases, Magical Mindset, Talk Nicely to Yourself, Practice Mirror Work and Learn the "Choose Again" method.

CHAPTER 6 – BE GRATEFUL EVERY DAY
An Attitude of Gratitude is a Superpower, Make a "Delights Jar" and other Gratitude Games.

CHAPTER 7 – SUPERCHARGE YOUR ENERGY
Energy Boosters and Energy Drainers, Energy Boosting with Friends & Family. Helpful Habits, A 1-2-3 Magical Morning

CHAPTER 8 – YOU'VE GOT THIS
How to use this book. Fun! Fun! Fun! Find Your Tribe, Make Magic A Habit, Your "Magical Me" Challenge

ALL YOUR MAGICAL FINGER-TAPS

Image Thank You – Norbert Buchholz

CHAPTER 1 - A LIFE THAT MAKES YOU FEEL LIGHT AND HAPPY

The best way to feel light and happy is to raise your energy through Magical Magnetising.

Image Thank You – Norbert Buchholz

THE LAW OF ATTRACTION

A big help for us all in Magical Magnetising is something called the Law of Attraction. It is based on the simple rule of *"what you think about comes about"*

This means that we create our real life through our imagination, so:
- If we keep visualising and trying, we will be successful at whatever we do.
- We can be anything we want to be.
- We have the power to make our dreams come true, dreams like:

Landing the lead role in the school play.

Getting into the school football team.

Hitting the right note in choir practice.

Making a big improvement in an English test.

WHAT LIGHTS YOU UP?

Each of us is wonderfully unique. There is only one you, and you are happiest when you are the best that you can be. It is possible for anyone, including you, to get very good at (almost) anything. It is totally natural to want to fit in rather than risk everyone laughing at you but be brave and don't worry what others think. You won't learn anything new, or become good at things, if you are so worried about looking daft that you don't even try.

If you want to be a fantastic footballer, astronaut, pianist, heart surgeon, ballet dancer, plumber, barista, teacher, vlogger, chef, fireman, prime minister, mathematician, celebrity presenter, actor, pop star, celebrity endorser, farmer, street magician, stunt skateboarder, cupcake baker or anything else that is on your heart, you need to tap into the magic inside you.

"Did you know that two-thirds of kids in school today will end up doing a job that hasn't even been invented yet? That is truly mind-boggling" (From "You Are Awesome" by Matthew Syed)

SOMETHING MAGICAL FOR YOU

I have created some great "MAGICAL FINGER-TAPS" which are a really simple way to help calm your anxiety or power up your happy. They involve touching the tips of your fingers with your thumb whilst saying some special words. Pressing the thumb and fingers together stimulates your brain, which then receives a signal to change the energy flow within your body.

You can use MAGICAL FINGER-TAPS anytime and anyplace, saying the words out loud and bold, quietly, or in your head depending on what you feel like doing at the time.

Put the tip of your thumb to the tip of your pointing finger when you say the first word, then move to the tip of your middle finger when you say the second word, to the tip of your ring finger for the third word and the tip of your pinkie when you say the last word.

MAGICAL FINGER-TAP
LIFE # LIGHTS # ME # UP

LIFE	LIGHTS	ME	UP
1	2	3	4
Thumb to pointing	Thumb to middle	Thumb to ring	Thumb to pinkie

Image Thank You – Freddie Molyneux

Keep repeating a MAGICAL FINGER-TAP for as long as it gives you energy and feels good to do.

I have popped some MAGICAL FINGER-TAPS throughout the book to help you remember the "Magical Me" messages and then there is a special list of them all plus others at the end. Enjoy!

CHAPTER 2 - IT'S THE LAW!

THE LAWS

According to Science there are certain Laws that govern the Universe:
- The Law of Gravity: what goes up must come down.
- Einstein's Law of Relativity: everything in the Universe is made of energy.
- The Law of Vibration: everything in the Universe vibrates; everything has its own vibe.
- The Law of Attraction: the most powerful law of them all, based on the simple rule of *"like attracts like"*, an ancient idea which was first thought of by the philosopher Plato as early as 391 BC.

MAGICAL FINGER-TAP
LIKE # ATTRACTS # LIKE # ENERGY

THE IMPORTANCE OF YOUR THOUGHTS

A great way of visualising *"like attracts like"* and understanding the importance of your thoughts, is by looking at the work of Japanese scientist Dr. Masaru Emoto in his book "The Hidden Messages in Water"
Using high-speed photography, Dr. Emoto discovered that crystals formed in frozen water reveal changes when specific, concentrated thoughts are directed toward them. He found

that water which has been exposed to loving words shows brilliant, complex, and colourful snowflake patterns. In contrast, water exposed to negative thoughts, forms incomplete, asymmetrical patterns with dull colours.
See the difference between a crystal which had the thought *"You Fool"* directed towards it, versus one which had received the thought of *"Thank You"*

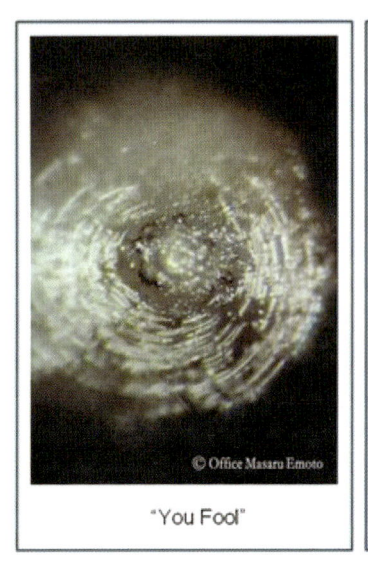

"You Fool"   "Thank You"

Image Thank You – Dr. Masaru Emoto

This quote from Roald Dahl's "The Twits" that perfectly sums up the importance of our thoughts.

"If a person has ugly thoughts, it begins to show on the face. And when that person has ugly thoughts every day, every week, every year, the face gets uglier and uglier until you can hardly

bear to look at it. A person who has good thoughts cannot ever be ugly. You can have a wonky nose and a crooked mouth and a double chin and stick-out teeth, but if you have good thoughts, they will shine out of your face like sunbeams, and you will always look lovely"

MAGICAL FINGER-TAP
LOVELY # THOUGHTS # LOVELY # FACE

FAMOUS MAGICAL MAGNETISING FANS

JK Rowling wrote her first book in a coffee shop with her baby daughter asleep in a pram next to her. She was unemployed and broke. 12 publishers rejected her manuscript. 12 turned down Harry Potter! She believed in the Law of Attraction and luckily a small editor saw the magic on her lucky 13th attempt. Never ever give up on your dream – this is big time Magical Magnetising in action.

There are many other famous Magical Magnetising fans like Jay-Z, Lady GaGa, Oprah Winfrey, Will Smith, Serena Williams**,** Conor McGregor, and Denzel Washington, who all know the importance of their thoughts and use them to attract a wonderful life.

MAGICAL FINGER-TAP
MY # THOUGHTS # BECOME # THINGS

Image Thank You – Julia August

AN IMPORTANT WORD ABOUT MIS-TAKES

A great way to think about it is as a "Mis-Take" in the movie of your life. You are the director of that movie, and you simply go back and do the take again – just as successful Movie Directors do.

When a challenge arises don't see it as an obstacle to be ignored, don't give up, put up a fight to be a bit better. Try, try, try again. Ask yourself what's the worst that can happen? Learn from it, learn from setbacks along the way.

You will be following in the successful footsteps of these "Famous Failures"

Michael Jordan, **Basketball Superstar** – *"I've missed more than 9000 shots in my career. I've lost almost 300 games, 26 times I've been trusted to take the game-winning shot and I missed. I've failed over and over again in my life….. and that is why I succeed"*

Thomas Edison, Inventor of the lightbulb - *"I haven't failed. I just found 10000 ways that didn't work."*

Serena Williams, Tennis Legend – *"I really think a champion is defined not by their wins but how they can recover when they fail"*

Steve Jobs, Founder of Apple – *"I'm convinced that about half of what separates successful entrepreneurs from the non-successful ones is pure perseverance."*

JK Rowling, Bestselling Author – *"It is impossible to live without failing at something, unless you live so cautiously that you might as well not have lived at all – in which case, you fail by default"*

MAGICAL FINGER-TAP
I # CAN # DO # IT

CHAPTER 3 - THE MAGIC MAGNET INSIDE YOU

THE POWER OF LOVE

Energy vibrates in waves called frequencies. Everything that happens to us in our body or in our heart or in our mind has its own vibrational frequency.

All your emotions are vibrations, where "love" is the highest and most powerful, and "hate" is the lowest. Your thoughts are vibrations or energy waves too with their own frequency which are attracted to other energy waves of the same frequency.

It's just like having a Magic Magnet inside you. So that is why *"what you think about comes about"* and why if you are a happy magnet from right inside your heart, you will attract happy things.

MAGICAL FINGER-TAP
MAGIC # MAGNET # INSIDE # ME

HEARTFUL BREATHING – 5 MINUTES EVERY DAY

Heartful Breathing is for both adults and children and brings together Mindfulness, Meditation, and Magical Magnetising in one simple practice which recharges you and gives the body rest far deeper than sleep.

**STOP
heart connect
RE-ENERGISE**

10 minutes. Every day. For life.

Image Thank You – Freddie Molyneux

What You Do

Take a deep breath and rub your palms together until they are warm. This opens your heart energy.

Put your lead hand (the one that you write with comfortably) on your heart centre in the middle of your chest. Then place your other hand, palm up in your lap, ready to receive Universal Energy.

Breathe slowly and deeply, in through your nose and out through your mouth. In through your nose and out through your mouth. As you continue you will most likely feel a warm glow under your hand at your heart centre.

The First Minute – Mindfulness

This is to encourage you to connect with all your senses. Sight. Hearing. Touch. Taste. Smell.

Firstly, tune into the light and darkness through your closed eyes, you may see floating colours or dots or just a plain dark background. Any, and all are OK. Then become aware of the loudest and the softest sounds around you. Just notice them. Then the most noticeable & most gentle touches. It could be the rub of your clothes or for me often the dog on my lap as he settles down! Discover the taste in your mouth, it may be strong or just a hint of a taste. Then become aware of the strongest & weakest smell around you. You have now connected with all your senses.

The Next 3 Minutes - Meditation

This step is so simple and so powerful. Keep going with your Heartful Breathing and on your in-breath repeat the word *"Heartful"* silently to yourself for at least 3 minutes, or however long you are Heartful Breathing for today.

In through your nose whilst silently saying *"Heartful",* out through your mouth.

In through your nose whilst silently saying *"Heartful",* out through your mouth.

The Last Minute – Magical Magnetising

Say out loud or to yourself *"Universe I am so grateful for"* … and add one thing you really want to happen, big or small. Thanking the Universe, as if it has already happened, gets you into the energy to magnetise it to you.

This can be the same thing every day to really boost your magic around that desire, or it can change as often as you like.

The key to Magical Magnetising is to imagine it as if it were happening, really bring that vision to life, what can you see, what are the sounds around you, how bright are the colours, what are people saying to you and, particularly how does it feel, especially in your heart.

I really hope you enjoy this and try to find 5 minutes for it every day.

There is a longer 10-minute Heartful Breathing guidance recording on my website that your parent or carer may wish to listen to and share with you.

MAGICAL FINGER-TAP
HEARTFUL # BREATHING # EVERY # DAY

HEART ANCHORING

This is a way of powering up the impact of your Heartful Breathing.

Select a special little item like a special stone, a crystal, a small soft toy or a special blankie. This is your Heart Anchor. Hold it to your heart centre when you are Heartful Breathing.

Whilst you are Heartful Breathing the frequency of your vibration is at the highest level of unconditional love. That vibration is then transferred to your Heart Anchor which you can carry round with you or hold any time that you need to calm down or soothe yourself.

MAGICAL FINGER-TAP
ANCHOR # MY # HEART # ENERGY

ACUPRESSURE FOR ANXIETY

Acupressure is an ancient Chinese healing method that involves putting pressure with the fingers or thumbs on certain body points. Anxiety can block the flow of energy around your body like when you get a tight feeling in your chest or a sore head.

HT7 or Heart 7 is the point where your wrist forms a crease with your hand.

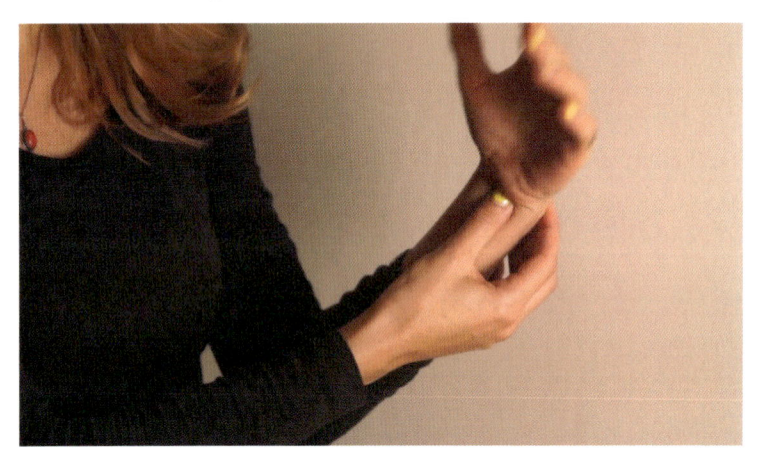

Image Thank You - YouTube

Take your thumb and apply firm pressure but not too much that it causes pain. Hold this pressure point and gently knead your thumb in a tight circular motion for about 2 minutes.

Do this to both wrists and your anxiety, stress and overall tension will come down immediately, whether you are at home, or school, or out.

MAGICAL FINGER-TAP
ACUPRESSURE # CALMS # ME # DOWN

CHAPTER 4 – GOODBYE UNHAPPY THOUGHTS

YOUR "LITTLE VOICE"

We all have a critical "Little Voice" inside, telling us that we are not good or smart or pretty or handsome or talented enough. That Little Voice is our fear and is trying to keep us safe. We always have a choice whether to listen to it or not.

Rather than letting it crowd your thoughts and stop you from doing things (or encouraging you to make wrong choices) it is a good idea to give your Little Voice a name. This is to separate it from you and gives you the choice of whether to listen to it. Don't overthink it – just the first name that comes into your head of someone, perhaps from a film or a book, who is critical or aggressive or not very kind. So, a name like Cruella (de Vil) or Bellatrix (Lestrange) ..... what will yours be?

Image Thank You – luchioly

Mine is called Fanny Anne and I try to get to know her because she represents my deeper thoughts. Then I say *"Thank you Fanny Anne for showing up today and keeping me safe. However, I have got this, and I don't need you so it's time for you to take a long holiday"*

Try naming your Little Voice, thanking them, and sending them on holiday and see how you get on.

MAGICAL FINGER-TAP
THANK # YOU # LITTLE # VOICE

YOUR "MONKEY MIND"

Steve Peters is a well-respected Professor and author of a great book "The Hidden Chimp". He specialises in how the human mind works. He says that in our "Monkey Mind" we have two parts of our brain that are used for thinking. When we are happy the blue brain, which we can control, is in charge. When we are upset the red brain, which we cannot control, is in charge. Acting without your permission, it can take over and make you do things that you don't want to do.

It is important to know that all feelings are normal, it is just that some are not helpful. These are the ones you get from your "Chimp" like telling lies, being mean to friends or family, being frightened of monsters under the bed or getting overanxious or worried all the time.

PARENT TIP

Always validate your child's feelings and help them put a name to their emotions. Once the emotion has passed, invite them to think about how they could handle it differently next time. Putting them in charge of the solution allows them to take responsibility for their own feelings and behaviour and empowers them to make better choices.

10 HABITS THAT MIGHT HELP YOU MANAGE YOUR CHIMP

Professor Peters advises:

1 Smiling. When you make yourself smile, it can make you feel happier. Think about good things in your life, something funny, people you like.

If you are sad underneath and can't smile, then decide when you want to be happy again.

Make a "Happy List" and do the things on it when you are ready.

2 Saying Sorry. This makes both the person you have upset, and you, feel better. Tell the truth; you will feel relieved that you don't need to cover it up anymore.

3 Being Kind. We all like it when someone is kind to us. Being kind to someone makes them happy and makes you feel good.

Help around the house; help if someone is in trouble; make friends by including them; say nice things about people; let people know that you like them; thank people for gifts or time or help; share and be kind to family or friends.

4 Talking about your Feelings. This helps you to understand them, especially if you are upset and that is very good for you.

Find someone who cares about you and will listen.

Talking about your feelings helps you to accept them and then you feel better every time you talk.

5 Asking for Help. It's good to try first, but then ask for support, as soon as you can't work something out. You will then you get things done more quickly and feel happier.

Even grown-ups ask for help

Most people are happy to help you.

6 Showing Good Manners. When you are polite, people feel happier and will like it. Being polite to others will make you feel good about yourself. It means respecting others and putting other people before yourself.

Give up your seat to someone more in need such as those who are older or pregnant.

Ask nicely; please may I have a drink, excuse me, do you mind if I say something.

Say thank you and mean it when people are nice.

7 Trying New Things. Different foods; a challenge; joining a group; looking after a pet; a new sport; playing an instrument; dancing; singing; or painting.

Our Chimps can be lazy or fearful and won't let us try new things.

When trying new things, our Chimps often give up too early.

Try new things with friends as Chimps like company.

8 Accepting when NO really means NO. Moaning, complaining and misbehaving isn't going to help. Once we accept that, then we can get on and be happy. Finding something else to do or talking to someone else will stop your Chimp grumbling and complaining.

9 Learning to Share. When we share, we look after others and make them happy. Think of what you can play or work on together; it is so much more fun with a friend.

10 Doing what you have to do whether you like it or not. Things like tidying up, getting ready for school, doing your homework, eating healthily, having a bath, cleaning your teeth, going to bed. It is best to make your Chimp get on with it and then you both feel great when you have finished. The secret is to do things immediately – count 5-4-3-2-1 and GO – and not give your Chimp a chance to think.

HELLO HAPPY THOUGHTS

Another great way to have a high vibe is to say goodbye to unhappy thoughts and hello to happy ones. Pick whichever of these "Goodbye and Hellos" work for you and say them to yourself regularly. It is helpful to associate this with an action to help you remember to do it – perhaps every time you have a drink or wash your hands?

Image Thank You – Norbert Buchholz

I Say Goodbye To: Unhappy thoughts.

I Say Hello To: Happy thoughts about big & small things.

I Say Goodbye To: Thinking people don't like me.

I Say Hello To: Knowing that the people who count really like me.

I Say Goodbye To: Thinking I don't look good, or my body isn't right.

I Say Hello To: Being happy in my skin, and knowing I am great just as I am.

I Say Goodbye To: Thinking school is hard and I can't do well.

I Say Hello To: Knowing there is lots of help at school and I am doing my very best.

I Say Goodbye To: Thinking I shouldn't tell an adult when someone is bullying or hurting me.

I Say Hello To: Knowing that telling a trusted adult is the best thing to do to keep me safe.

I Say Goodbye To: Thinking I'm not perfect.

I Say Hello To: Knowing that no-one is perfect, that the best people learn from mistakes.

I Say Goodbye To: Thinking my dreams are stupid or won't come true.

I Say Hello To: Thinking I can attract a happy and wonderful life.

I Say Goodbye To: Anything mean or hurtful that anyone has ever done to me.

I Say Hello To: Enjoying this moment in this day with joy and hope.

I Say Goodbye To: Feeling that I am no good and everyone else is better than me.

I Say Hello To: Knowing that we all have different strengths and when I do what lights me up, I will fly.

I Say Goodbye To: Being tired all the time.

I Say Hello To: Good habits which help me to bounce with energy.

MAGICAL FINGER-TAP
HELLO # TO # HAPPY # THOUGHTS

A NEGATIVITY CLEAN UP

This is another great thing to raise your energy: a promise to yourself to stop criticising, talking meanly about others, complaining, or moaning. Or at least if you catch yourself doing it, even thinking it in your head, then try and stop yourself.

The energy that most of us waste on doing this can really make us unhappy and drag down our vibe. According to the Law of Attraction, the Universe doesn't know the difference, and delivers whether it is something you want or something you don't want. So, if we..........

Complain - we give ourselves something more to complain about.

Moan - we give ourselves something more to moan about.

Criticise - we give ourselves something more to be critical about.

Please give this Negativity Clean Up a try every day for a week at least and notice how much better it makes you feel.

MAGICAL FINGER-TAP
NO # MOANING # OR # COMPLAINING

Image Thank You – Crazy nook

CHAPTER 5 - POSITIVE THOUGHTS ATTRACT POSITIVE THINGS

YOU ARE ALWAYS ATTRACTING

You are always vibrating and attracting experiences and things at the same vibration. Whether you know it or not, whether it is brilliant or not very nice at all.

An example would be the perfect free kick that you visualise bending into the top corner and in your next game, guess what, it does. Or a song that you like, which is stuck in your head, and it keeps coming on the radio. Or being worried that someone in your friendship group doesn't like you and then you start to fall out.

If you think and believe negative things like *"I am not as good as everyone else"* or *"everyone has things I want"* you will attract negative experiences. Similarly, if you think positive things like *"I am so lucky"* then that is what you will attract.

When you ask the Universe for what you want it is important to use positive language, focus on what you DO want, not what you DON'T want. And it is great as if you can imagine it as if it is happening, so saying *"I AM"*

Rather than saying Universe *"I DON'T want to be lonely in the playground"*, say *"Universe, I DO want to be popular and nice to everyone......I AM popular and nice to everyone"*

And really feel in your heart what it feels like for that to happen. Please remember that passion and excitement are so important in lifting your energy.

Then be patient and trust the Universe to deliver at the right moment and for the good of everyone.

And most importantly do remember to say, *"Thank You Universe"*

MAGICAL FINGER-TAP
POSITIVE # THOUGHTS # POSITIVE # THINGS

POSITIVE PHRASES

These are incredibly powerful to have in your Help-Yourself Toolbox! They are short, uplifting, and motivational phrases that help you say what you want out of life and feel good.

So, you can pull any of these out and say them out loud to yourself whenever you need a lift in a particular area.

I have also given you a lovely MAGICAL FINGER-TAP for each area too.

LOVE YOURSELF

"I came into this world to make a difference and be happy"

"Beautiful and handsome come in all shapes, sizes and colours, and I am perfect as I am"

"If I love myself then it is easy for others to love me too"

"I am a good friend to myself"

"I am buzzing that life loves me and I love life"

"I am important, and I believe in me"

MAGICAL FINGER-TAP
PERFECT # AS # I # AM

STAND TALL

"Saying NO means that I am strong"

"No-one can make me feel bad. I have the power to be positive about me"

"Only brave people ask for help. I am brave"

"If anyone tries to hurt me with words or actions I talk to my parents or carers or teachers"

"I stand up for what is important to me. It doesn't matter what anyone else thinks"

MAGICAL FINGER-TAP
STAND # TALL # AND # STRONG

BE A GOOD FRIEND

"I am popular because I am friendly to everyone"

"I find it easy to make friends"

"I try not to hurt others or say or do mean things"

"I care about me and others (and animals and nature and the environment)"

MAGICAL FINGER-TAP
I'M # LOVING # AND # JOYFUL

Image Thank You – TairA

LIKE SCHOOL

"I am happy in school and love seeing my friends"

"Every day and in every way, I do my best at school"

"I embrace difference and enjoy learning about all kinds of customs and beliefs"

"I am happy to ask for help"

MAGICAL FINGER-TAP
I # DO # MY # BEST

STAY CALM

"I am calm, and I know everything will be fine"

"I move on quickly from what might happen"

"If something goes wrong, I will learn from it"

"I am safe, and I am protected"

When I feel anxious or scared or angry, I do Heartful Breathing and feel better"

MAGICAL FINGER-TAP
TODAY'S # A # GREAT # DAY

ACT KINDLY

"I tell the truth"

"I help others in need and am a good listener"

"I do the right thing, treating others how I would like to be treated"

"I love to share"

"I am nice to myself and others and know that kindness changes the world"

MAGICAL FINGER-TAP
KINDNESS # CHANGES # THE # WORLD

BE HEALTHY

"I eat and drink things that are good for me"

"I love fun movement and exercise, to take good care of my body and me"

"I get outside every day in fresh air"

"I feel great, I look great, I am great"

"I am healthy, and it feels so good"

"I am strong and feel very well"

MAGICAL FINGER-TAP
I # AM # SUPER # HEALTHY

HAPPY VIBES

"I deserve happy, I am happy"

"I think happy thoughts"

"Life is fun, I smile, I laugh, I love being alive"

"I am born to be great and have a happy life"

"I spend time every day being grateful"

"I feel alive with energy"

"I have a happy, wonderful life"

MAGICAL FINGER-TAP
HAPPY # HAPPY #HAPPY # ME

MAGICAL MINDSET

Mindset is the way we look at the world and our place in it. If you have a "Fixed or STUCK Mindset" it can hold you back (such as thinking you can only be good if you are born that way). Or you can choose a "Growth or MAGICAL Mindset" where you believe that you can become good at things.

STUCK Mindset Thoughts

"My sister is the brainy one out of us"

"I often start things but never finish them"

"We are all hopeless at singing in our family"

"My co-ordination is rubbish. I will never be able to play tennis"

"Everyone in the class is way better than me at Maths, I just don't get it"

MAGICAL Mindset Thoughts – this is one of the biggest secrets to a happy life

"It makes sense to have a go at anything. Putting effort in is the only way to get better at stuff"

"Ability can be changed with practice. Talents, gifts, and skills can be developed"

"I welcome a challenge. Bring It On! Trying new things is the only way to learn. I don't mind if I don't get it right first time. That's fine. I'll get it next time and the time after that"

"Mis-takes happen. They are nothing to be ashamed of. They show me exactly what I don't know so that I can work on improving my skills"

"I appreciate feedback. Unless I know where I am going wrong, I will never be able to improve"

"I always try to find out how others achieved their goals. What did they do? How can I do the same to achieve success?"

"I know that I can train my brain which is a mental muscle"

What MAGICAL Mindset really looks like

Belief # Open-Minded # Being Positive # Practice # Effort # Confidence # Making Loads of Mis-Takes # Learning Again and Again # Challenging Yourself

Image Thank You - Lja/Dreamstime

TALK NICELY TO YOURSELF

Alongside your Negativity Clean Up around others, it is important to be kind to yourself too. We talk to ourselves constantly and the relationship that we have with ourselves is the most important one of all. Your words, to yourself and others, are like seeds which you plant in the soil of your mind.

When was the last time that you were lovely to yourself, talked kindly to yourself and believed what you said in your heart?

You are with yourself 24/7. So, make what you are saying to you, kind, inspiring and uplifting. This will help you to be happy and have high energy.

A SPECIAL WORD ABOUT SOCIAL MEDIA

"Comparisonitis is the robber of dreams" (Donna and Cheryl from Now is Your Time)

Some people constantly compare their looks or lives to other air brushed fake lives, especially those of celebrities. Then they feel jealous, sad, like they are missing out and just not good enough. It is a sure-fire way to lower your energy which we know we need to keep nice and high because *"like attracts like energy"*

So, if you view any social media do it selectively, limit how often, and think very carefully about how it may be affecting you.

MAGICAL FINGER-TAP
NICE # KIND # SELF # TALK

Image Thank You – Rolau Elena

REFLECTIONS IN THE MIRROR

The mirror is a great place to help you talk nicely to yourself.

Every morning for at least a month really look at yourself in the mirror first thing in the morning. Look deeply into your eyes and repeat this statement 10 times (or a statement of your choosing).

"I love myself. I am great inside and out. I let go of any negative self-talk"

Most people find this difficult to start with, but it does get easier. It really transforms how kind you are to yourself, and therefore everyone else around you.

MAGICAL FINGER-TAP
GREAT # INSIDE # AND # OUT

THE "CHOOSE AGAIN" METHOD

A most helpful method for changing negative thought patterns is from a great spiritual leader and author called Gabby Bernstein. She says the moment that you feel wobbly, notice your thought, thank the thought, then "Choose Again" – what is the best feeling thought that I can feel right now?

Take what is worrying you and confront it with changed thinking and evidence to back that up by completing the sentence RIGHT NOW……………………

For example, if you are feeling jealous of a friend who has loads of money and stuff....

RIGHT NOW......I have running water, heat and food.

RIGHT NOW.... I have love from my friends.

RIGHT NOW....I know that being happy is far more important than stuff.

Then ask the Universe to guide you towards that new thought whilst saying this prayer: *Thank-you Universe for guiding my thoughts towards feel good emotions.*

MAGICAL FINGER-TAP
CHOOSE # THAT # THOUGHT # AGAIN

Image Thank You – TairA

CHAPTER 6 – BE GRATEFUL EVERY DAY

AN "ATTITUDE OF GRATITUDE"

Buddha says *"It is not happy people who are thankful, it is thankful people who are happy"*

The superpower of gratitude is a real game-changer and lifts your vibration. A grateful heart only gives more to be grateful for.

An "Attitude of Gratitude" means making it a habit to express sincere thanks and appreciation in all parts of your life, on a regular basis, for both the big and small things that we experience. Gratitude has a powerful ability to shift and raise vibrations. The more grateful you are, the stronger the heart connection and therefore the higher your energy.

If you concentrate on what you have, you'll always have more. If you concentrate on what you don't have, you'll never have enough. Simple.

Focusing on what you're grateful for tends to wash away feelings of anger and negativity and helps us to connect to our heart and raise our vibration.

Having an "Attitude of Gratitude" is one of the most impactful habits for a fulfilling, healthy and positive life.

MAGICAL FINGER-TAP
MY # ATTITUDE # IS # GRATITUDE

Image Thank You – Norbert Buchholz

BE GRATEFUL EVERY DAY

Every day, please write down 3 things that you are grateful for AND the reason WHY. You can do this on bits of paper, or your nice "Magical Me Journal"/ decorated exercise book.

The writing down helps you to focus your thinking, gives your gratitude a stronger energy and allows you to read them back at any time.

The "WHY" allows you to go much deeper into the feeling and becomes the magnet. For example.

"I am so grateful for walks in the park with my family because it makes me feel brighter and we get to chat"

"I am very grateful for my new smiley faces water bottle because it is fun and reminds me to drink at least 4 bottles a day – which I know is so good for me"

"I am really grateful for my next-door neighbour because he is a friend outside school. It is good to have friends from different places and we have lots of laughs"

Do your best to include different things every day and be as imaginative as you can. But most importantly, HAVE FUN.

MAGICAL FINGER-TAP
WAKE-UP # AND # BE # GRATEFUL

A DELIGHTS JAR

A further idea is to write your Gratitudes on a separate sheet, cut them up and put them folded into a "Delights Jar" (ask for an old, washed jar which you can label)

Anytime you need a lift dive into the "Delights Jar" and re-read them for some feel goods. You know your family best – they may also join in and do this with you.

MAGICAL FINGER-TAP
DELIGHTS # EVERY # SINGLE # DAY

Image Thank You - Shafran

OTHER GRATITUDE GAMES

Be Grateful for Family & Friends. Take it in turns with a family member or friend to say something you are grateful for and why until you exhaust your list but energise your heart.

Be Grateful for You. Congratulate yourself for what you have done and achieved in your life, however big or small, and what you are grateful for about yourself.

Be Grateful for Others. Acknowledge other people and thank them for inspiring, helping and supporting you.

Be Grateful to The Universe. Regularly thank the universe for all your blessings (or God or Allah or Buddha or a Higher Power – whatever you feel happy with)

Another great idea is to read "Have You Filled a Bucket Today?" by Carol MCleod; a heart-warming book recommended by a teacher friend. It encourages positive behaviour by using the concept of an invisible bucket to show children how easy and rewarding it is to express kindness, gratitude, appreciation, and love by "filling buckets." It explains that it's possible to fill or dip into our own buckets, which is a choice.

MAGICAL FINGER-TAP
I # AM # SO # GRATEFUL

CHAPTER 7 – SUPERCHARGE YOUR ENERGY

The most important thing to help you live a life that lights you up is looking after your energy, as well as creating more of it.

ENERGY BOOSTERS AND ENERGY DRAINERS

You are your own power station and need to keep topping it up.

STEP 1 - Ask yourself what is one thing that you can do and then keep adding to that.

The thing I'm going to do more of to boost my physical energy daily is.......

For example, stretches for 10 minutes every day.

The thing I'm going to do more of to boost my emotional energy daily is.......

For example, Heartful Breathing every single day.

STEP 2 – Ask yourself what is one thing that you can stop doing and then keep adding to that.

The thing I can see that drains my energy is......

For example, getting involved in lots of rows with a child in my class.

What I'm going to do to remove that energy drainer is......

For example, count to 10 before I say anything and try to be kind and calm.

MAGICAL FINGER-TAP
HEART # ENERGY # POWERS # ME

ENERGY BOOSTING WITH FRIENDS AND FAMILY
Outdoor activities: such as climbing trees, swimming, cycling, making dens, building dams, crabbing, fishing, bug hunting, collecting shells, rock pooling, just playing and not having adults supervising too closely. Trying these builds confidence and resilience and keeps mind and body healthy.

Passion activity: What is yours? You don't have to be the best at it but 'doing' an activity such as craft, sport, computer games, cooking, art, skateboarding etc) takes the mind away from anxieties that are real. Immersing yourself in your passion can make you happy and raise your vibe.

Image Thank You – luchioly

Board games: give you the chance to talk, stop, relax, and think. This is a great one where you can work together on a problem, openly discuss friendship and families, anger, anxiety, and social topics without any pressure.
'A really good game is 'Thinkfun Rush Hour – Traffic Jam Logic, Brain & Challenge Game' available from Amazon and other retailers'

MAGICAL FINGER-TAP
 I'M # FILLED # WITH # ENERGY

HELPFUL HABITS

Habits are the practices, routines, or behaviours that we perform regularly, often without thinking. We tend to have 'bad' or 'good' habits.

Which habits do you currently have which work well for you? Name the Top 3
1
2
3

What habits do you have that you want to break? Name the Top 3
1
2
3

Right now, what is the Number 1 habit you want to break in order for you to be the best you?

And how are you going to do that/ who can help you?

MAGICAL FINGER-TAP
HELPFUL # HABITS # HIGH # ENERGY

1-2-3 MAGICAL MORNING

The first hour of your day is so important to help you have a Magical Life. Here are some great helps to get into an amazing routine.

1-2-3 MAGICAL MORNING

WHILST STILL IN BED

1 Heart Connection: Start each day with your hands on your heart and say the Buddhist prayer to yourself *'May I be filled with loving kindness. May I be well. May I be peaceful and at ease. May I be happy'*. Really listen to what your heart says.

Image Thank You – Norbert Buchholz

2 Wishes: How do you want to show up today? What energy are you choosing to bring today? What good can you do today? In your mind, run through a couple of key things that are going to happen in your day, and how they will happen super positively.

3 Gratitudes: Think of 3 things you are grateful for and WHY

THEN ONCE UP (BEFORE YOU TOUCH ANY TECHNOLOGY!)

Music & Movement – blast out your favourite song(s) and crazy dance as if no-one is watching. Or do some stretches or jog on the spot or kick a ball in the garden. Do whatever is your thing and mix it up when you get bored. This will raise your energetic vibration.

Heartful Breathing – highly recommended for at least 5 minutes every day.

MAGICAL FINGER-TAP
MAGICAL # MORNING # MAGICAL # DAY

CHAPTER 8 – YOU'VE GOT THIS

FUN! FUN! FUN!

If you make feeling good the most important thing, you will magnetise more good things to you. Ask yourself:

"What can I do to have that feel great feeling?"

"What is the one thing I should focus on?"

"What is the best next step to take?"

One of the most important messages of this whole book, and for life itself, is to HAVE FUN along the way! For just about everyone, the goal is to be HAPPY – when we have these feelings inside, we don't need the material stuff.

When your goal is to feel good, you become a magnet for what you want. Plus, your joyful high vibe energy ripples out and lifts-up everyone around you.

Image Thank You – Norbert Buchholz

FIND YOUR TRIBE

You Do You. The best way to be more joyful is to spend time doing things you like. Living a life that lights you right up is what "Magical Me" is all about.

Ask yourself where can I have more fun? What makes me feel good/ feel alive? Sit and do your own quick-fire list of things that light you up and do your best to make sure that you do some of them regularly.

It is good to learn to do things you like by yourself, as well as finding your tribe to lift your energy and have fun with. Family, school friends, neighbours, others at a dance club, people who support the same team - it can be a couple of people or loads – anyone who gets you and you get them.

If you don't feel that you have a tribe, then try and start with being a friendly and approachable person. Remember, "*what you give out you get back*". Give out friendly, positive vibes and you're more likely to receive the same back. A smile or a friendly word cost nothing and can mean everything.

MAGICAL FINGER-TAP
FUN # IS # THE # MAGIC

MAKE MAGIC A HABIT

It takes 21 days to form a new habit, so let's rate your energy. Give yourself a score from 1 – 5 and write it in your Journal now….. and, again at end of 21 days.

1 – Fed up, flat and sad

2 – Sort of OK but not much energy and a bit sad

3 – Enough energy but I would like more, sometimes happy sometimes sad

4 – Generally happy and more than enough energy to do things

5 – Super happy and loads of energy, pretty much always bouncy

YOUR "MAGICAL ME" CHALLENGE

This is not homework it is Magic Work. I have made lots of helpful, fun suggestions throughout this book which will help you to have your most Magical Life.

In addition to Daily Heartful Breathing, think of 3 things from this book that sound good to you and try your best to keep to doing them every day for 21 Days. It is a really good idea to write down what you think you can do and to tell a grown up so they can support you. So, for example:

I, Wendy Molyneux, am committing to doing Daily Heartful Breathing and these 3 things for the next 21 days – from today's date xx/xx/xx to 21 days' time – yy/yy/yy

1. **Name My "Little Voice"** – *thank it and send it on holiday every time it pops up to criticise me.*
2. **Gratitudes** – *write down 3 every day (and start a "Delights Jar")*
3. **Mirror Reflection** - *first thing in the morning look deeply into my eyes and repeat this 10 times - "I love myself. I am great inside and out. I let go of any negative self-talk"*

Then in 21 days score yourself again and stop and think how you are now feeling, what has changed and how Magical Life is.

You can continue with these suggestions, add some more, mix them up, do whatever is on your heart, whatever lights you up.

Image Thank You – Passiflora

MAGICAL FINGER-TAPS

This is a special list for you to keep coming back to as often as you like. What I find fun is to close my eyes and let my finger be guided to point at a MAGICAL FINGER-TAP. Or choose a number randomly in your head and look up which one it is. That is then the MAGICAL FINGER-TAP which is meant for you in that moment to give you a positive boost.

1. A # CIRCLE # OF # LOVE
2. ALL # IS # REALLY # WELL
3. ANCHOR # MY # HEART # ENERGY
4. DELIGHTS # EVERY # SINGLE # DAY
5. EXPRESS # THOUGHTS # AND # FEELINGS
6. FOLLOW # MY # WISDOM # INSIDE
7. FREE # AS # A # BIRD
8. FRESH # AIR # POWERS # ME
9. GO # WITH # THE # FLOW
10. GOOD # FOOD # NURTURES # ME
11. GOOD # IN # MY # LIFE
12. GREAT # INSIDE # AND # OUT
13. HAPPY # HAPPY #HAPPY # ME
14. HEART # ENERGY # POWERS # ME
15. HEARTFUL # BREATHING # EVERY # DAY
16. HELLO # TO # HAPPY # THOUGHTS
17. HELPFUL # HABITS # HIGH # ENERGY
18. I # ACCEPT # MY # SELF
19. I # ACCEPT # OTHER # PEOPLE
20. I # AM # ALWAYS # SAFE
21. I # AM # AT # EASE
22. I # AM # MAGICAL # ME
23. I # AM # MOST # MAGICAL
24. I # AM # PERFECTLY # PROTECTED
25. I # AM # REALLY # BLESSED
26. I # AM # SO # GRATEFUL
27. I # AM # SUPER # HEALTHY
28. I # AM # WORTH # LOVING
29. I # CAN # DO # IT
30. I # CHOOSE # MY # THOUGHTS
31. I # CREATE # LOVELY # BELIEFS
32. I # CREATE # MY # LIFE
33. I # DO # MY # BEST
34. I # HAVE # A # CHOICE

35 I # HAVE # LIMITLESS # POTENTIAL
36 I # HAVE # SUPER # POWERS
37 I # LOVE # BEING # ME
38 I # LOVE # MY # FAMILY
39 I # LOVE # MY # FRIENDS
40 I # LOVE # MY # LIFE
41 I # LOVE # MYSELF # ALWAYS
42 I # LOVE # MYSELF # LOTS
43 I # REALLY # FORGIVE # MYSELF
44 I # REALLY # FORGIVE # OTHERS
45 I # REALLY # TRUST # MYSELF
46 I # SAY # POSITIVE # THINGS
47 I # SLEEP # REALLY # DEEP
48 I # THINK # POSITIVE # THINGS
49 I # TRUST # MY # THOUGHTS
50 I # VIBRATE # WITH # LIGHT
51 I'M # A # YES # PERSON
52 I'M # FILLED # WITH # ENERGY
53 I'M # HAPPY # WITH # CHANGE
54 I'M # HAPPY # WITH # ME
55 I'M # LIGHT # AND # LOVE
56 I'M # LOVED # AND # SAFE
57 I'M # LOVING # AND # JOYFUL
58 I'M # ME # AND # FREE
59 I'M # MY # BEST # FRIEND
60 I'M # TRUE # TO # ME
61 I'M # WILLING # TO # CHANGE
62 IN # HARMONY # WITH # NATURE
63 IT'S # ONLY # A # THOUGHT
64 JUST # PERFECT # AS # ME
64 KINDNESS # CHANGES # THE # WORLD
66 LET # MY # LIGHT # SHINE
67 LET # NASTY # THOUGHTS # GO
68 LET # THE # LOVE # IN

69	LIFE # CARES # FOR # ME
70	LIFE # FULL # OF # JOY
71	LINKED # TO # THE # UNIVERSE
72	LISTENING # TO # MY # HEART
73	LOVE # KNOWS # NO # BOUNDS
74	LOVE # MORE # RECEIVE # MORE
75	LOVE # SHINES # BRIGHT # WITHIN
76	MAGIC # MAGNET # INSIDE # ME
77	MAGICAL # MAGICAL # MAGICAL # ME
78	MAGICAL # MORNING # MAGICAL # DAY
79	MAKING # THE # RIGHT # CHOICES
80	MY # ATTITUDE # IS # GRATITUDE
81	MY # HOME # IS # PEACEFUL
82	MY # WORDS # ARE # POWERFUL
83	NEW # LEARNING # EVERY # DAY
84	NO # MOANING # OR # COMPLAINING
85	PEACE # AT # MY # CENTRE
86	PEACE # IN # MY # HEART
87	PEACE # IN # MY # MIND
88	PEOPLE # WELCOME # MY # IDEAS
89	PERFECT # AS # I A# AM
90	RICH # IN # EVERY # WAY
91	SAFE # SECURE # AND # LOVED
92	SAYING # NO # IS # FINE
93	STAND # TALL # AND # STRONG
94	THANK # YOU # LITTLE # VOICE
95	THOUGHTS # CAN # BE # CHANGED
96	TODAY'S # A # NEW # DAY
97	TODAY'S # A # GREAT # DAY
98	UNIVERSAL # POWER # IS EVERYWHERE
99	WAKE-UP # AND # BE # GRATEFUL
100	WILLINGLY # LEARNING # NEW # THINGS

JUST TO REMIND YOU

You can use MAGICAL FINGER-TAPS anytime and anyplace, saying the words out loud and bold, quietly, or in your head depending on what suits you at the time.

Put the tip of your thumb to the tip of your pointing finger when you say the first word, then move to the tip of your middle finger when you say the second word, to the tip of your ring finger for the third word and the tip of your pinkie when you say the last word.

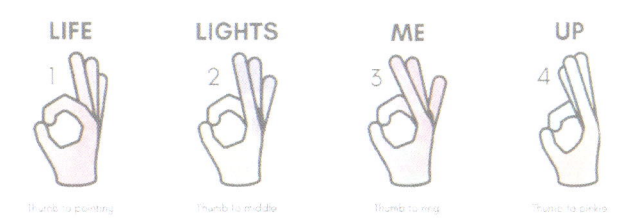

LIFE	LIGHTS	ME	UP
1	2	3	4
Thumb to pointing	Thumb to middle	Thumb to ring	Thumb to pinkie

Image Thank You – Freddie Molyneux

Keep repeating your MAGICAL FINGER-TAP for as long as it gives you energy and feels good to do.

Be Happy. Be Calm. Be Magical.

Wendy xxx

The Heartfulness Coach™

DISCLAIMER

The information in this book is for general purposes and nothing contained in it is, or is intended to be, construed as therapeutic advice. It is not a substitute for medical examination, diagnosis, attention, or treatment and is not intended to take the place of proper advice from a fully qualified practitioner.

Copyright C 2021 – Wendy Molyneux
All rights reserved

No part of this book may be reproduced in any form or by any electronic or mechanical means, including information storage and retrieval systems, without written permission from the author, except for the use of brief quotations in a book review.

The Heartfulness Coach™ is a registered trademark.

Printed in Great Britain
by Amazon